DOGS

LABRADOR RETRIEVERS

by Elizabeth Andrews

Cody Koala
An Imprint of Pop!
popbooksonline.com

Hello! My name is Cody Koala

This book is filled with videos, puzzles, games, and more! Scan the QR codes* while you read, or visit the website below to make this book pop.

popbooksonline.com/labrador-ret

*Scanning QR codes requires a web-enabled smart device with a QR code reader app and a camera.

abdobooks.com

Published by Pop!, a division of ABDO, PO Box 398166, Minneapolis, Minnesota 55439.

Printed in the United States of America, North Mankato, Minnesota.

102022
012023

THIS BOOK CONTAINS RECYCLED MATERIALS

Cover Photo: Shutterstock Images
Interior Photos: Shutterstock Images; Getty Images; Elizabeth Andrews
Editor: Grace Hansen
Series Designer: Colleen McLaren

Library of Congress Control Number: 2022941103

Publisher's Cataloging-in-Publication Data
Names: Andrews, Elizabeth, author.
Title: Labrador retrievers / by Elizabeth Andrews
Description: Minneapolis, Minnesota : Pop!, 2023 | Series: Dogs | Includes online resources and index.
Identifiers: ISBN 9781098243227 (lib. bdg.) | ISBN 9781098243920 (ebook)
Subjects: LCSH: Labrador dogs--Juvenile literature. | Retrievers--Juvenile literature. | Sporting dogs--Juvenile literature. | Domestic Dog--Juvenile literature.
Classification: DDC 636.752--dc23

Table of Contents

Chapter 1

America's Favorite Breed

Labrador retrievers, Labs for short, are often the most popular dog **breed** in the United States. Their brains and beauty are just two reasons they are so beloved!

Watch a video here!

chocolate

yellow

black

Labs are medium sized dogs. They are strong and sturdy. Their coat is short, straight, and **dense**. It can be black, yellow, or chocolate in color.

A Labrador has a **broad** head with powerful jaws. Its ears flop forward and hang close to its face. A Lab's tail is

thick at the base and **tapers** down to the end. The tail is good for swimming.

Labs' eyes range from brown to hazel in color. The dogs have very kind eyes.

Chapter 2

Lovely Labs

Labs are gentle and loving dogs. They are very smart and **even-tempered**. They get along well with anyone. Labs like to be a part of the action and need lots of love and attention.

Learn more here!

Labs were originally **bred** to hunt in water. Their strong sense of smell also helps them hunt in fields. Over time they became popular family pets. But the dogs kept their high energy and love for the water.

Labs should have toys to chew on and play with to help release energy.

Today, Labs are given many jobs besides hunting. Since they are smart, they can be trained in search and rescue and various service jobs. They even work in the military!

MARIA
Ultra Paws
Ultra Paws
Ultra Paws

Chapter 3

Dog Care

Labs have a lot of energy. It is the owner's job to find activities for their dog. Labs should be exercised daily. They like to run and swim. They are also great fetch players.

After being in water, a Lab's ears should be dried out. This can prevent ear infections.

Explore links here!

A Lab's coat needs occasional brushing and baths. The nails should be kept short. Labs need healthy food and plenty of fresh water. Owners should take their Lab to the vet for regular checkups.

Chapter 4

Puppies

Lab puppies are born deaf and blind. They gain their senses at ten to 14 days old. At eight weeks old, puppies are ready to be **adopted**! Training should start right away.

Complete an activity here!

Making Connections

Text-to-Self

What color Labrador retriever would you want?

Text-to-Text

Have you read any books about other retrieving dogs? If so, how were those dogs similar to or different from the Labrador retriever?

Text-to-World

Look closer into what service jobs Labradors can do. Which do you think are the most important? Explain your answer.

Glossary

adopted – taken in as a pet.

bred – developed to act and look a specific way, or serve a certain purpose.

breed – a particular type or kind of animal.

broad – wide and large.

dense – having parts very close together with little space between.

even-tempered – not easily upset or made angry.

taper – to become thinner at one end.

Index

Online Resources

popbooksonline.com

Thanks for reading this Cody Koala book!

This book is filled with videos, puzzles, games, and more! Scan the QR codes* while you read, or visit the website below to make this book pop.

popbooksonline.com/labrador-ret

*Scanning QR codes requires a web-enabled smart device with a QR code reader app and a camera.